© Copyright 2024 Mount Everest Hold reserved.

The contents of this book may not be reproduced, duplicated or transmitted without direct written permission from the author or the publisher.

Under no circumstances will any legal responsibility or blame be held against the publisher, or author, for any reparation, damages, or monetary loss due to the information contained within this book, either directly or indirectly.

Legal Notice:

This book is copyright protected. This is only for personal use. You cannot amend, distribute, sell, use, quote or paraphrase any part or the content within this book without the consent of the author.

Disclaimer Notice:

Please note the information contained within this document is for educational and entertainment purposes only. Every attempt has been made to provide accurate, up to date, reliable and complete information. No warranties of any kind are expressed or implied. Readers acknowledge that the author is not engaging in the rendering of legal, financial, medical or professional advice. The content of this book has been derived from various sources.

By reading this document, the reader agrees that under no circumstances is the author responsible for any losses, direct or indirect, which are incurred as a result of the use of information contained within this document, including, but not limited to, errors, omissions, or inaccuracies.

Table Of Contents

Disclaimer Notice: 8
Chapter 1: Introduction to Caviar Pairing 8
    The History of Caviar 8
    The Importance of Pairing Caviar with Champagne and Wine 8
Chapter 2: Understanding Caviar Varieties 8
    Beluga Caviar 8
    Osetra Caviar 8
    Sevruga Caviar 8
    American Sturgeon Caviar 8
Chapter 3: Champagne Pairing with Caviar 8
    Brut Champagne 8
    Blanc de Blancs Champagne 8
    Rosé Champagne 8
    Vintage Champagne 8
Chapter 4: Wine Pairing with Caviar 8
    Chardonnay 8
    Sauvignon Blanc 8
    Pinot Noir 8
    Sparkling Wine 8
Chapter 5: Tips for Perfect Caviar Pairing 8
    Serving Suggestions 8
    Temperature and Storage 8
    Presentation and Garnishes 8

Chapter 6: Hosting a Caviar Pairing Party 8
   Setting the Mood 8
   Pairing Menu Ideas 8
   Caviar Tasting Notes 8
Chapter 7: Exploring New Caviar and Wine Pairings 8
   Experimental Pairings 8
   Regional Pairings 8
   Customizing Your Pairings 8
Chapter 8: Conclusion and Resources 8
   Final Thoughts 8
   Additional Reading and Resources 8
   Glossary of Terms 8
Chapter heading page 8
Sensory Impact: The Delicate Nature of Caviar 8
Oxidation and Metallic Taste 8
Texture and Temperature 8
Tradition and Aesthetics: The Cultural Significance 8
Non-Metal Alternatives 8
Historical Context 8
Practical Considerations: Enhancing the Caviar Experience 8
Cost and Investment 8
Ritual and Appreciation 8
Conclusion: Respecting the Delicacy 8
The Health Benefits of Eating Fine Caviar 8
Nutritional Profile of Caviar 8
Cardiovascular Health 8
Omega-3 Fatty Acids and Heart Health 8
Antioxidant Properties 8
Brain Health 8
Cognitive Function and Mental Health 8
Eye Health 8
Prevention of Age-Related Macular Degeneration 8
Improvement in Dry Eye Syndrome 8
Bone Health 8
Vitamin D and Calcium Absorption 8
Phosphorus and Bone Strength 8
Immune System Support 8
Vitamin A 8
Selenium and Zinc 8

Skin Health 8
Omega-3 Fatty Acids and Skin Hydration 8
Vitamin E and Antioxidant Protection 8
Anti-Inflammatory Benefits 8
Reduction of Inflammatory Markers 8
Muscle and Joint Health 8
Protein for Muscle Repair and Growth... 8
Omega-3s and Joint Health... 8
Reproductive Health 8
Omega-3s and Fertility 8
Vitamins and Minerals for Reproductive Health............................ 8
Weight Management... 8
Satiety and Appetite Control 8
Conclusion 8
The World of Fine Caviar: Types, Prices, and What Makes Them Special 8
The Basics of Caviar... 8
Types of Caviar by Sturgeon Species... 8
Beluga Caviar 8
Characteristics 8
Price and Rarity 8
Top Varieties 8
Osetra Caviar 8
Characteristics 8
Price and Popularity.. 8
Sevruga Caviar 8
Characteristics 8
Price and Accessibility 8
Kaluga Caviar 8
Characteristics 8
Price and Market... 8
Sterlet Caviar 8
Characteristics 8
Price and Availability 8
Siberian Sturgeon Caviar.. 8
Characteristics 8
Price and Popularity.. 8
American Sturgeon Caviar 8
Characteristics 8

- Price and Market 8
- Factors Influencing Caviar Prices 8
- Species and Rarity 8
- Maturation Time 8
- Quality and Grading 8
- Farming and Sustainability 8
- Conclusion 8
- The Proper Way to Serve Fine Caviar: Dishes, Etiquette, and Presentation 8
- The Basics of Serving Caviar 8
- Storing Caviar 8
- Choosing the Right Utensils 8
- Presentation 8
- Traditional Accompaniments 8
- Blini 8
- Crème Fraîche 8
- Toast Points and Crackers 8
- Hard-Boiled Eggs 8
- Onions and Chives 8
- Lemon Wedges 8
- Creative Serving Ideas 8
- Caviar Canapés 8
- Sushi and Sashimi 8
- Deviled Eggs 8
- Caviar Tartlets 8
- Pairing Caviar with Beverages 8
- Champagne 8
- Vodka 8
- White Wine 8
- Caviar Etiquette 8
- Serving Etiquette 8
- Eating Etiquette 8
- Social Etiquette 8
- Regional Variations and Specialties 8
- Russian Caviar Traditions 8
- Iranian Caviar Traditions 8
- French Caviar Traditions 8
- Japanese Caviar Traditions 8
- American Caviar Traditions 8

Detailed Serving Suggestions 8
Elegant Caviar Platters 8
Caviar Tasting Events 8
Gourmet Caviar Dishes 8
Understanding Caviar Quality 8
Caviar Grading 8
Recognizing Freshness 8
The Cultural Significance of Caviar 8
Historical Importance 8
Modern Luxury 8
Ethical and Sustainable Caviar 8
Hosting a Caviar Tasting at Home 8
Planning and Preparation 8
Conducting the Tasting 8
Etiquette and Enjoyment 8
Conclusion 8
Books 8
Online Resources 8
Articles and Journals 8
Conclusion 8
Legal Notice: 1

Chapter 1: Introduction to Caviar Pairing

The History of Caviar

The history of caviar is a fascinating tale that dates back centuries. Caviar, the salt-cured roe of the sturgeon fish, has long been considered a delicacy fit for royalty and the elite. The origins of caviar can be traced back to ancient Persia, where it was enjoyed by the ruling class as a symbol of wealth and prestige. Over time, caviar spread throughout Europe and Russia, becoming a coveted luxury item among the aristocracy.

In the 19th century, caviar gained popularity in Western Europe and the United States, where it became a staple at high-end restaurants and luxurious banquets. Russian caviar, particularly from the Beluga sturgeon, was highly sought after for its large, creamy eggs and rich flavor profile. However, overfishing and pollution led to a decline in sturgeon populations, making genuine caviar increasingly rare and expensive.

Today, caviar is produced in several countries, including Russia, Iran, and the United States. Sustainable farming practices have helped to preserve sturgeon populations and ensure the continued availability of high-quality caviar. Caviar connoisseurs now have a wide variety of options to choose from, including Beluga, Osetra, and Sevruga caviar, each with its own unique flavor profile and texture.

Pairing caviar with champagne or wine is a time-honored tradition that can enhance the flavors of both the food and drink. The effervescence of champagne helps to cleanse the palate between bites of rich, salty caviar, while the acidity and fruitiness of wine can complement the briny notes of the roe. When choosing a wine or champagne to pair with caviar, it's important to consider the specific type of caviar being served, as well as personal preferences for flavor profiles.

In conclusion, the history of caviar is a rich tapestry of tradition, luxury, and culinary excellence. Caviar connoisseurs can appreciate the time-honored techniques used to harvest and cure this prized delicacy, as well as the sustainable practices that ensure its continued availability. Pairing caviar with champagne and wine is a sensory experience that can elevate the flavors of both the food and drink, creating a truly luxurious dining experience for those with discerning tastes.

The Importance of Pairing Caviar with Champagne and Wine

For caviar connoisseurs, the art of pairing this delicacy with the right champagne and wine is crucial in order to fully appreciate its flavors and textures. The combination of caviar with champagne and wine can elevate the tasting experience, creating a harmonious balance that enhances the overall enjoyment of the meal. In this subchapter, we will explore the importance of pairing caviar with champagne and wine, and provide some tips and guidelines for creating the perfect pairing.

One of the main reasons why pairing caviar with champagne and wine is so important is that the acidity and effervescence of these beverages can help to cut through the richness of the caviar, balancing out its intense flavor and texture. Champagne, with its crisp bubbles and refreshing acidity, is a classic choice for pairing with caviar, as it cleanses the palate and enhances the flavors of the caviar. Similarly, a dry white wine or a light-bodied red wine can also complement the briny and buttery notes of caviar, creating a delightful contrast that enhances the overall tasting experience.

Another reason why pairing caviar with champagne and wine is important is that the right beverage can bring out the nuances and subtleties of the caviar, allowing you to fully appreciate its complexity and depth of flavor. The acidity in champagne and wine can enhance the salty and savory notes of the caviar, while the effervescence can help to open up the palate and enhance the overall tasting experience. By carefully selecting the right champagne or wine to pair with your caviar, you can create a truly memorable dining experience that will delight your senses and leave you craving more.

When it comes to pairing caviar with champagne and wine, it is important to consider the quality and characteristics of both the caviar and the beverage in order to create a harmonious balance. The texture, flavor profile, and intensity of the caviar should be taken into account when selecting a champagne or wine to pair with it, as certain combinations can enhance or detract from the overall tasting experience. Experimenting with different pairings and finding the perfect match for your caviar can be a fun and rewarding experience, allowing you to discover new flavors and sensations that you may not have noticed before.

In conclusion, the importance of pairing caviar with champagne and wine cannot be overstated for caviar connoisseurs. The right combination of caviar with the appropriate champagne or wine can elevate the tasting experience, bringing out the best qualities of both the caviar and the beverage. By carefully selecting and experimenting with different pairings, you can create a truly memorable dining experience that will delight your senses and leave you craving more. So next time you indulge in caviar, be sure to pour yourself a glass of champagne or wine to enhance the flavors and textures of this luxurious delicacy.

Chapter 2: Understanding Caviar Varieties

Beluga Caviar

Beluga caviar, often referred to as the "king of caviar," is one of the most prized and sought-after delicacies in the world of gourmet food. Known for its large, luscious pearls and rich, buttery flavor, beluga caviar is a favorite among caviar connoisseurs for its exquisite taste and luxurious texture. Beluga caviar comes from the beluga sturgeon, a species native to the Caspian and Black Seas. These sturgeons can grow to be incredibly large, with some reaching lengths of up to 20 feet and weighing over 2,000 pounds.

The flavor profile of beluga caviar is often described as creamy, nutty, and slightly briny, with a smooth, velvety texture that melts in your mouth. The color of beluga caviar can range from pale gray to deep black, depending on the age of the sturgeon and the quality of the eggs. Beluga caviar is prized for its distinct taste and luxurious mouthfeel, making it a favorite pairing for fine wines and champagnes.

When pairing beluga caviar with champagne, it is important to choose a champagne that is crisp, dry, and effervescent to complement the rich, buttery flavor of the caviar. Brut champagne or a Blanc de Blancs champagne are ideal choices, as they provide a refreshing contrast to the creamy texture of the caviar. The bubbles in champagne also help to cleanse the palate between bites, allowing you to fully appreciate the complex flavors of the caviar.

For those who prefer wine to champagne, a light, crisp white wine such as Chardonnay or Sauvignon Blanc can also make a wonderful pairing with beluga caviar. The acidity and fruitiness of these wines help to enhance the flavors of the caviar without overpowering them, creating a harmonious balance of taste sensations. When choosing a wine to pair with beluga caviar, opt for a high-quality, well-balanced wine that complements the luxuriousness of the caviar.

In conclusion, beluga caviar is a true delicacy that deserves to be savored and enjoyed in the company of fine wines and champagnes. Whether you prefer the crisp, refreshing bubbles of champagne or the light, fruity notes of a white wine, there is a perfect pairing waiting to be discovered. By experimenting with different combinations and finding the perfect match for your palate, you can elevate your caviar tasting experience to new heights of luxury and sophistication. Cheers to the art of caviar pairing!

Osetra Caviar

Osetra caviar is one of the most sought-after varieties of caviar in the world, known for its rich, nutty flavor and delicate texture. This prized delicacy comes from the Osetra sturgeon, which is native to the Caspian and Black Seas. The eggs are typically medium to large in size, with a distinct golden to dark brown color that can vary depending on the age of the sturgeon and the region in which it was harvested.

When it comes to pairing Osetra caviar with champagne or wine, there are a few key factors to consider. The first is the crispness and acidity of the beverage. Champagne, with its effervescence and bright acidity, is a classic choice for pairing with Osetra caviar. The bubbles help to cleanse the palate between bites of the rich caviar, while the acidity cuts through the fat and enhances the flavors of the eggs.

Another important consideration when pairing Osetra caviar with champagne or wine is the flavor profile of the beverage. Osetra caviar has a nutty and buttery flavor that pairs well with wines that have similar characteristics, such as Chardonnay or Pinot Noir. These wines have a richness and complexity that complement the caviar without overpowering it, allowing the delicate flavors of the eggs to shine through.

When serving Osetra caviar, it is important to do so with care and attention to detail. The caviar should be served chilled but not frozen, as extreme temperatures can alter the texture and flavor of the eggs. It is best to serve the caviar on a bed of ice or chilled serving dish to maintain its freshness and ensure that it stays at the optimal temperature for enjoyment.

In conclusion, Osetra caviar is a luxurious and decadent delicacy that pairs beautifully with champagne and wine. By considering the crispness, acidity, and flavor profile of the beverage, as well as serving the caviar with care and attention to detail, caviar connoisseurs can create a truly unforgettable dining experience that showcases the exquisite flavors of Osetra caviar at their best.

Sevruga Caviar

Sevruga caviar, also known as the "black gold of the Caspian Sea," is a highly sought-after delicacy among caviar connoisseurs. This type of caviar comes from the Sevruga sturgeon, a species known for its small, delicate eggs and rich, briny flavor. Sevruga caviar is often prized for its intense taste and creamy texture, making it a favorite choice for pairing with champagne and wines.

One of the key factors that sets Sevruga caviar apart from other types of caviar is its distinctive flavor profile. The eggs are smaller and darker in color, with a bold, earthy taste that can range from mild to robust depending on the age of the sturgeon. The creamy texture of Sevruga caviar also adds to its appeal, allowing it to melt in your mouth and release a burst of flavor with each bite.

When it comes to pairing Sevruga caviar with champagne and wines, there are a few key things to keep in mind. The briny, umami-rich flavor of the caviar pairs beautifully with the crisp acidity and effervescence of champagne, making it an ideal choice for special occasions and celebrations. For a classic pairing, opt for a dry champagne or sparkling wine with a high acidity to complement the richness of the caviar.

For those who prefer wine, Sevruga caviar can also be paired with a variety of white wines, such as Chardonnay or Sauvignon Blanc. The crisp, citrusy notes of these wines help to enhance the flavor of the caviar without overpowering it, creating a harmonious balance of flavors that will delight your palate. When choosing a wine to pair with Sevruga caviar, look for a bottle with a bright acidity and subtle fruit flavors to complement the briny taste of the caviar.

In conclusion, Sevruga caviar is a luxurious and versatile delicacy that pairs beautifully with both champagne and wines. Its bold flavor and creamy texture make it a favorite among caviar connoisseurs, who appreciate its unique taste and elegant presentation. Whether enjoyed on its own or paired with your favorite bubbly or white wine, Sevruga caviar is sure to elevate any dining experience and leave a lasting impression on your taste buds.

American Sturgeon Caviar

American Sturgeon Caviar is a delicacy that has been gaining popularity among caviar connoisseurs in recent years. This type of caviar is known for its rich, buttery flavor and delicate texture, making it a perfect pairing for champagne and wines. American Sturgeon Caviar is sourced from the sturgeon fish native to North America, particularly the waters of the Great Lakes and the Mississippi River.

One of the key characteristics of American Sturgeon Caviar is its unique flavor profile. The caviar has a mild, nutty taste with a hint of brininess, which pairs beautifully with the effervescence of champagne and the complex flavors of wines. The buttery texture of the caviar also adds a luxurious mouthfeel to any pairing, enhancing the overall sensory experience.

When pairing American Sturgeon Caviar with champagne, it is important to choose a crisp and dry variety to complement the richness of the caviar. Brut Champagne or Blanc de Blancs are excellent choices, as they provide a refreshing contrast to the buttery texture of the caviar. The acidity of the champagne helps to cleanse the palate between bites, allowing the flavors of the caviar to shine through.

For wine pairings, opt for a light and crisp white wine such as Sauvignon Blanc or Chardonnay. These wines have a bright acidity that complements the nutty and briny notes of the caviar, creating a harmonious balance of flavors. Additionally, the citrusy and floral aromas of these wines enhance the overall tasting experience, making each bite of caviar a true delight for the palate.

In conclusion, American Sturgeon Caviar is a luxurious and versatile delicacy that pairs beautifully with champagne and wines. Its rich flavor profile and buttery texture make it a perfect addition to any caviar pairing experience. By choosing the right champagne or wine to accompany the caviar, caviar connoisseurs can elevate their tasting experience and enjoy the intricate flavors of this gourmet treat to the fullest.

Chapter 3: Champagne Pairing with Caviar

Brut Champagne

In the world of luxury dining, nothing quite compares to the exquisite pairing of caviar with champagne. And when it comes to champagne, one of the most revered varieties is Brut Champagne. Known for its crisp, dry taste and effervescent bubbles, Brut Champagne is the perfect complement to the rich and delicate flavors of caviar.

Brut Champagne is a type of champagne that is known for its low sugar content, making it the driest of all champagne varieties. This dryness allows the natural flavors of the champagne to shine through, making it an ideal pairing for the salty and briny taste of caviar. The bubbles in Brut Champagne also help to cleanse the palate between bites of caviar, allowing you to fully appreciate the nuances of both the champagne and the caviar.

When pairing Brut Champagne with caviar, it is important to choose a high-quality champagne that has been aged properly. Look for a champagne that has been aged for at least three years, as this will help to enhance the complexity of the flavors and ensure a smooth and elegant finish. Additionally, be sure to serve the champagne chilled, as this will help to accentuate the crispness of the bubbles and enhance the overall tasting experience.

In terms of specific caviar pairings, Brut Champagne is particularly well-suited to traditional varieties such as Beluga, Osetra, and Sevruga. These types of caviar have a rich and buttery flavor profile that is beautifully complemented by the crisp and refreshing taste of Brut Champagne. The pairing of these two decadent delicacies is sure to impress even the most discerning caviar connoisseur.

In conclusion, Brut Champagne is a luxurious and sophisticated choice for pairing with caviar. Its dryness, effervescence, and clean finish make it the perfect accompaniment to the rich and delicate flavors of caviar. So next time you indulge in a serving of your favorite caviar, be sure to pour yourself a glass of Brut Champagne and savor the exquisite combination of flavors. Cheers to the art of caviar pairing!

Blanc de Blancs Champagne

Blanc de Blancs Champagne is a luxurious and elegant choice for caviar connoisseurs looking to elevate their tasting experience. Made exclusively from Chardonnay grapes, this type of champagne is known for its crisp acidity, delicate flavors, and bright, citrusy notes. Its light and refreshing profile pairs perfectly with the rich, salty taste of caviar, creating a harmonious balance of flavors on the palate.

The purity and finesse of Blanc de Blancs Champagne make it an ideal companion for a variety of caviar types, from the classic Beluga to the more delicate Osetra and Sevruga. The champagne's effervescence helps to cleanse the palate between bites, allowing the subtle nuances of each caviar variety to shine through. Its minerality and toasty undertones provide a sophisticated backdrop for the intense flavors of the caviar, enhancing the overall tasting experience.

When selecting a Blanc de Blancs Champagne to pair with caviar, look for bottles from renowned Champagne houses such as Ruinart, Salon, or Taittinger. These producers are known for their exceptional quality and craftsmanship, ensuring a memorable and indulgent caviar tasting experience. Opt for a vintage Blanc de Blancs Champagne for added complexity and depth, as the extended aging process imparts additional layers of flavor and nuance to the wine.

To fully appreciate the marriage of Blanc de Blancs Champagne and caviar, serve the champagne chilled in flute glasses to preserve its effervescence and delicate aromas. Pair it with a selection of premium caviar varieties, accompanied by traditional accompaniments such as blinis, crème fraîche, and finely chopped red onions. The combination of the crisp, refreshing champagne and the rich, creamy caviar is a match made in culinary heaven, creating a sensory experience that is sure to delight even the most discerning caviar connoisseurs.

In conclusion, Blanc de Blancs Champagne is a sophisticated and versatile choice for pairing with caviar, offering a perfect balance of flavors and textures that elevate the tasting experience to new heights. Whether enjoyed as a standalone indulgence or as part of a luxurious caviar tasting menu, this exquisite champagne is sure to impress and delight even the most discerning palates. Cheers to the art of caviar pairing with Blanc de Blancs Champagne!

Rosé Champagne

Rosé Champagne is a luxurious and elegant choice for pairing with caviar. The delicate pink hue of Rosé Champagne comes from the addition of a small amount of red wine during the blending process, giving it a unique and complex flavor profile that complements the briny richness of caviar perfectly. Caviar connoisseurs will appreciate the subtle notes of red fruit, citrus, and floral aromas that Rosé Champagne brings to the palate, enhancing the overall dining experience.

When pairing caviar with Rosé Champagne, it is important to consider the quality of both the caviar and the champagne. Opt for a high-quality Rosé Champagne that is well-balanced and has a fine mousse, as this will enhance the flavors of the caviar and create a harmonious pairing. Look for caviar that is fresh, flavorful, and sustainably sourced, as this will ensure that you are getting the best possible taste experience.

One of the key reasons why Rosé Champagne is such a popular choice for pairing with caviar is its versatility. Rosé Champagne can be paired with a wide range of caviar types, from the delicate and buttery Osetra to the bold and briny Beluga. The effervescence and acidity of Rosé Champagne help to cleanse the palate between bites of caviar, allowing you to fully appreciate the nuances of both the champagne and the caviar.

For the ultimate caviar pairing experience, consider serving Rosé Champagne in a chilled flute alongside a selection of caviar on a bed of ice. This presentation not only looks stunning but also helps to keep the champagne and caviar at the perfect temperature for enjoyment. As you savor each bite of caviar and sip of Rosé Champagne, take the time to appreciate the intricate flavors and textures that make this pairing so special.

In conclusion, Rosé Champagne is a fantastic choice for pairing with caviar, offering a luxurious and sophisticated taste experience for caviar connoisseurs. With its delicate pink hue, complex flavor profile, and versatility, Rosé Champagne enhances the flavors of caviar and creates a memorable dining experience. So next time you indulge in a serving of caviar, be sure to reach for a glass of Rosé Champagne to elevate your tasting experience to new heights. Cheers to the art of caviar pairing!

Vintage Champagne

Vintage Champagne is a true delight for caviar connoisseurs. The term "vintage" refers to champagne made from grapes harvested in a single specified year. These champagnes are crafted with the utmost care and attention to detail, resulting in a truly exceptional and unique flavor profile. Vintage champagnes are often aged for longer periods of time, allowing the flavors to develop and mature, creating a complex and nuanced taste that pairs beautifully with the delicate flavors of caviar.

When pairing vintage champagne with caviar, it is important to consider the characteristics of both the champagne and the caviar. Vintage champagnes tend to have a more pronounced acidity and minerality, which can complement the rich and briny flavors of caviar. The effervescence of the champagne also helps to cleanse the palate between bites of caviar, allowing you to fully appreciate the flavors of both the champagne and the caviar.

One of the key factors to keep in mind when pairing vintage champagne with caviar is the age of the champagne. Older vintage champagnes tend to have a more developed and complex flavor profile, with notes of brioche, toasted nuts, and dried fruits. These flavors can enhance the buttery and nutty notes of caviar, creating a truly decadent pairing experience. Younger vintage champagnes, on the other hand, may have more vibrant fruit flavors and a crisp acidity that can provide a refreshing contrast to the richness of the caviar.

Vintage champagne is a versatile pairing option for caviar connoisseurs, as it can complement a wide range of caviar varieties, from the delicate and buttery Osetra to the bold and briny Beluga. Whether you prefer a Blanc de Blancs made from 100% Chardonnay grapes or a Blanc de Noirs made from Pinot Noir and Pinot Meunier grapes, there is a vintage champagne out there to suit your taste preferences. Experimenting with different vintage champagnes and caviar pairings can be a fun and rewarding experience, allowing you to discover new and exciting flavor combinations that will elevate your caviar tasting experience to new heights.

Chapter 4: Wine Pairing with Caviar

Chardonnay

Chardonnay is a versatile and popular wine choice for caviar pairing among connoisseurs. Its crisp acidity and subtle fruit flavors complement the delicate taste of caviar, making it an excellent choice for enhancing the overall dining experience. Chardonnay is a white wine that is typically aged in oak barrels, giving it a rich and creamy texture that pairs beautifully with the buttery texture of caviar.

One of the key factors to consider when pairing Chardonnay with caviar is the style of the wine. Chardonnays can range from light and crisp to full-bodied and oaky, so it's important to choose a bottle that will complement the flavor profile of the caviar. For example, a light and unoaked Chardonnay pairs well with delicate and mild caviars, while a full-bodied and oaky Chardonnay is better suited for more robust caviars like Osetra or Sevruga.

When selecting a Chardonnay for caviar pairing, it's also important to consider the region where the wine was produced. Chardonnay is grown in many different regions around the world, each with its own unique terroir that influences the flavor of the wine. French Chardonnays from regions like Burgundy and Chablis are known for their mineral-driven flavors, while California Chardonnays are often fruit-forward and oaky.

For a truly decadent caviar pairing experience, consider serving your Chardonnay slightly chilled to bring out its crisp acidity and refreshing qualities. The cool temperature of the wine will also help to cleanse the palate between bites of caviar, allowing you to fully appreciate the complexity of both the wine and the caviar. Whether you prefer a classic French Chardonnay or a bold California style, pairing it with caviar is sure to elevate your dining experience to new heights.

Sauvignon Blanc

Sauvignon Blanc is a white wine varietal that is beloved by many caviar connoisseurs for its crisp acidity and vibrant flavors. This wine is known for its herbaceous notes, with hints of green bell pepper, grass, and citrus. The bright acidity of Sauvignon Blanc makes it a perfect pairing for caviar, cutting through the rich, buttery flavors of the roe and cleansing the palate with each sip.

One of the key reasons Sauvignon Blanc pairs so well with caviar is its ability to enhance the delicate flavors of the roe without overpowering them. The wine's herbaceous notes complement the briny, oceanic flavors of the caviar, creating a harmonious balance on the palate. Additionally, the crisp acidity of Sauvignon Blanc helps to cleanse the palate between bites, allowing you to fully appreciate the nuances of the caviar.

When selecting a Sauvignon Blanc to pair with your caviar, look for a wine that is unoaked and has bright acidity. Wines from regions such as Marlborough in New Zealand or the Loire Valley in France are known for their vibrant acidity and herbaceous flavors, making them excellent choices for caviar pairings. Serve your Sauvignon Blanc chilled to enhance its refreshing qualities and ensure that it complements the caviar perfectly.

For a truly decadent caviar pairing experience, consider serving your Sauvignon Blanc alongside blinis topped with crème fraîche and a dollop of caviar. The creamy texture of the crème fraîche and the salty pop of the caviar pair beautifully with the crisp acidity of the wine, creating a luxurious and indulgent flavor combination. Whether you're hosting a special occasion or simply treating yourself to a gourmet meal, Sauvignon Blanc is sure to elevate your caviar pairing experience to new heights.

In conclusion, Sauvignon Blanc is a versatile and elegant choice for pairing with caviar. Its crisp acidity and herbaceous notes complement the delicate flavors of the roe, creating a harmonious balance on the palate. When selecting a Sauvignon Blanc for your caviar pairing, look for a wine with bright acidity and unoaked flavors. Whether you're enjoying caviar with blinis or simply savoring it on its own, Sauvignon Blanc is sure to enhance the experience and elevate your taste buds to new heights.

Pinot Noir

Pinot Noir is a versatile and elegant red wine that pairs perfectly with caviar, making it a favorite among caviar connoisseurs. Known for its light to medium body, high acidity, and complex flavors, Pinot Noir enhances the delicate taste of caviar without overpowering it. Its earthy notes and fruity undertones complement the briny and buttery flavors of the luxurious delicacy, creating a harmonious and unforgettable pairing experience.

One of the reasons why Pinot Noir is such a popular choice for caviar pairing is its ability to balance the richness of the caviar with its bright acidity and subtle tannins. This allows the wine to cleanse the palate between bites, preparing it for the next indulgent mouthful of caviar. The smooth and silky texture of Pinot Noir also adds a luxurious touch to the overall tasting experience, making it a perfect match for the refined and sophisticated flavors of caviar.

When selecting a Pinot Noir to pair with caviar, look for wines from cooler climate regions such as Burgundy, Oregon, or New Zealand. These wines tend to have higher acidity and more pronounced fruit flavors, which complement the delicate taste of caviar beautifully. Opt for a well-aged Pinot Noir with soft tannins and a complex flavor profile to elevate the pairing to new heights and create a memorable dining experience for you and your guests.

To truly appreciate the art of caviar pairing with Pinot Noir, take the time to savor each bite of caviar and sip of wine slowly. Pay attention to how the flavors of the caviar and wine interact on your palate, and notice how each enhances and elevates the other. Experiment with different types of caviar and Pinot Noir wines to discover your personal favorite pairing, and don't be afraid to get creative with your combinations to find the perfect match for your taste preferences.

In conclusion, Pinot Noir is a sophisticated and versatile wine that pairs beautifully with caviar, making it a popular choice among caviar connoisseurs. Its bright acidity, smooth texture, and complex flavors enhance the delicate taste of caviar, creating a harmonious and luxurious pairing experience. By selecting a well-aged Pinot Noir from a cooler climate region and taking the time to savor each bite and sip, you can truly appreciate the art of caviar pairing and elevate your dining experience to new heights.

Sparkling Wine

Sparkling wine is a luxurious and versatile beverage that pairs exceptionally well with caviar. The effervescence and acidity of sparkling wine cleanse the palate between bites of rich, briny caviar, allowing the delicate flavors of the roe to shine through. Whether you prefer Champagne, Prosecco, Cava, or any other type of sparkling wine, there is a perfect pairing waiting to be discovered.

When selecting a sparkling wine to pair with caviar, it is important to consider the style of the wine. Champagne, for example, is known for its complex flavors and fine bubbles, making it an excellent choice for pairing with high-quality caviar. Prosecco, on the other hand, is lighter and fruitier, making it a great match for more delicate varieties of caviar. Experimenting with different styles of sparkling wine can help you find the perfect pairing for your favorite type of caviar.

One of the key factors to consider when pairing caviar with sparkling wine is the level of saltiness in the caviar. Saltier caviar varieties, such as Osetra or Sevruga, pair well with a crisp, dry sparkling wine that can cut through the saltiness and enhance the flavors of the roe. Less salty caviar varieties, like Beluga or Sterlet, pair beautifully with a slightly sweeter sparkling wine that can complement the subtle flavors of the roe without overpowering them.

In addition to the saltiness of the caviar, the texture of the roe can also influence the choice of sparkling wine. Creamy, buttery caviar varieties, such as Beluga or White Sturgeon, pair well with a rich, full-bodied sparkling wine that can stand up to the luxurious texture of the roe. Lighter, more delicate caviar varieties, like Salmon or Trout, pair best with a crisp, refreshing sparkling wine that can enhance the delicate flavors of the roe without overwhelming them.

In conclusion, sparkling wine is a perfect companion for caviar, enhancing the flavors of the roe and cleansing the palate between bites. By considering the style, saltiness, and texture of the caviar, you can find the perfect pairing of sparkling wine to elevate your caviar tasting experience. Whether you prefer Champagne, Prosecco, or any other type of sparkling wine, there is a perfect pairing waiting to be discovered in the world of caviar and wine connoisseurship.

Chapter 5: Tips for Perfect Caviar Pairing

Serving Suggestions

Serving caviar is an art form, and the right accompaniments can enhance the experience of tasting this luxurious delicacy. When it comes to caviar pairing with champagne and wines, there are a few key considerations to keep in mind. In this subchapter, we will explore some serving suggestions to help you elevate your caviar tasting experience.

First and foremost, it is essential to serve caviar chilled. The delicate flavors of caviar are best enjoyed when the roe is kept at a cool temperature. To achieve this, place the container of caviar in a bowl of ice or in the refrigerator for at least 30 minutes before serving. Avoid freezing caviar, as this can alter its texture and flavor profile.

When it comes to serving caviar, simplicity is key. The flavor of caviar should be allowed to shine, so opt for neutral accompaniments such as blinis, toast points, or lightly buttered crackers. These simple bases provide a subtle background that allows the caviar to take center stage. Avoid using strong-flavored condiments or garnishes that may overpower the delicate taste of the roe.

In terms of champagne pairing, the effervescence and acidity of the bubbly can complement the rich and briny flavor of caviar. Opt for a dry champagne or sparkling wine, such as a brut or extra brut, to balance the saltiness of the caviar. The crisp acidity of the champagne helps to cleanse the palate between bites, allowing you to fully appreciate the nuances of the caviar.

For those who prefer wine pairing, a light and acidic white wine such as Chablis or Champagne is an excellent choice. The bright acidity of these wines can cut through the richness of the caviar, creating a harmonious balance of flavors. Alternatively, a dry rosé or a light-bodied red wine like Pinot Noir can also be a good match for caviar, providing a different flavor profile to explore.

In conclusion, serving caviar with champagne and wines is a sophisticated and luxurious experience that requires attention to detail. By following these serving suggestions, you can create a memorable tasting experience that highlights the unique flavors of caviar while complementing them with the perfect beverage pairings. Cheers to indulging in the art of caviar pairing!

Temperature and Storage

Temperature and storage are crucial factors to consider when it comes to preserving the delicate flavors of caviar. Caviar connoisseurs know that maintaining the right temperature is essential to ensure that the luxurious taste and texture of the roe are preserved. Ideally, caviar should be stored at a temperature between 28-32 degrees Fahrenheit to maintain its freshness and prevent it from spoiling. Storing caviar at a higher temperature can cause it to spoil quickly, while storing it at a lower temperature can freeze and damage the delicate eggs.

When it comes to storing caviar, it is important to keep it in its original packaging or a non-reactive container to prevent any unwanted odors or flavors from seeping into the delicate roe. Additionally, caviar should be stored in the coldest part of the refrigerator, such as the back or bottom shelf, to ensure a consistent temperature. It is also recommended to consume caviar within a few days of opening the container to ensure optimal freshness and flavor.

For caviar connoisseurs who are pairing their roe with champagne or wine, it is important to consider the temperature of both the caviar and the beverage. Champagne and white wines are best served chilled, while red wines are typically served at room temperature. When pairing caviar with champagne, opt for a brut or extra brut champagne that is dry and crisp to complement the salty and briny flavors of the caviar.

When serving caviar with wine, consider the flavor profile of the wine and how it will complement the delicate flavors of the roe. For example, a light and crisp white wine such as Chardonnay or Sauvignon Blanc can enhance the buttery texture of the caviar, while a bold and robust red wine such as Cabernet Sauvignon or Merlot can provide a rich and luxurious pairing. Experiment with different wine and caviar pairings to find the perfect combination that suits your palate and enhances the overall dining experience.

Presentation and Garnishes

Presentation and garnishes play a crucial role in enhancing the overall experience of enjoying caviar. As caviar connoisseurs, we understand the importance of not only selecting the finest quality caviar but also presenting it in a way that showcases its elegance and sophistication. When it comes to serving caviar, attention to detail is key.

One of the most common ways to present caviar is on a bed of crushed ice. This not only helps to keep the caviar chilled but also adds a touch of elegance to the presentation. Another popular option is to serve caviar on a mother-of-pearl spoon, which is believed to enhance the taste of the caviar. Some connoisseurs even prefer to serve caviar on a warm blini, adding a subtle contrast of temperatures and textures.

When it comes to garnishes, less is often more. Traditional accompaniments such as chopped chives, hard-boiled eggs, sour cream, and lemon wedges can complement the delicate flavor of caviar without overpowering it. Caviar can also be paired with toasted brioche or potato chips for added crunch and texture. The key is to choose garnishes that enhance the caviar without overshadowing its unique taste.

For those looking to elevate their caviar experience, consider experimenting with unconventional garnishes such as edible flowers, microgreens, or even gold leaf. These unexpected touches can add a sense of luxury and sophistication to your caviar presentation. Pairing caviar with the right champagne or wine can also enhance the overall experience, bringing out the nuances of both the caviar and the beverage.

In conclusion, presentation and garnishes are essential elements of caviar pairing that should not be overlooked. As caviar connoisseurs, we understand the importance of creating a visually stunning and delicious experience for our guests. By paying attention to the details of presentation and garnishes, we can elevate the enjoyment of caviar and create unforgettable moments for ourselves and our fellow connoisseurs.

Chapter 6: Hosting a Caviar Pairing Party

Setting the Mood

Setting the mood is an essential element when it comes to enjoying the exquisite delicacy of caviar paired with the perfect champagne or wine. As caviar connoisseurs, we understand the importance of creating an atmosphere that enhances the flavors and textures of this luxurious treat. Whether you are hosting a formal dinner party or simply indulging in a private tasting session, setting the mood is key to elevating the overall experience.

When it comes to setting the mood for a caviar pairing, ambiance is everything. Consider dimming the lights and lighting candles to create a warm and inviting atmosphere. Soft music playing in the background can also help to set the tone for a sophisticated and elegant dining experience. The goal is to create a space that allows you to fully appreciate the nuances of the caviar and the champagne or wine you have selected to pair with it.

In addition to ambiance, the table setting is also an important aspect of setting the mood for a caviar pairing. Opt for fine china and crystal glassware to showcase the elegance of the occasion. Fresh flowers or simple table decorations can add a touch of beauty to the setting. Pay attention to the details, such as using silver utensils and linen napkins, to create a refined and polished look that complements the indulgent nature of caviar and champagne.

Another key element of setting the mood for a caviar pairing is the selection of the champagne or wine itself. Consider the flavor profiles of the caviar you will be serving and choose a champagne or wine that will complement those flavors. Whether you prefer a crisp and refreshing champagne or a rich and full-bodied wine, the right pairing can elevate the experience and bring out the best in both the caviar and the beverage.

Overall, setting the mood for a caviar pairing is about creating a sensory experience that allows you to fully appreciate the flavors, textures, and aromas of these luxurious delicacies. By paying attention to the ambiance, table setting, and beverage selection, you can create a dining experience that is truly unforgettable for you and your guests. So take the time to set the mood and savor every moment of your caviar pairing experience.

Pairing Menu Ideas

For the discerning caviar connoisseur, the perfect pairing can elevate the dining experience to a whole new level. When it comes to pairing caviar with champagne and wine, there are endless possibilities to explore. From the classic combination of champagne and caviar to the more adventurous pairings with different types of wines, the key is to find the perfect balance of flavors to complement the delicate taste of the caviar.

One classic pairing that never fails to impress is champagne and caviar. The effervescence of the champagne enhances the rich, buttery flavor of the caviar, creating a harmonious blend of flavors that is simply irresistible. For a truly decadent experience, try pairing a vintage champagne with a high-quality caviar for a match made in heaven.

If you're looking to experiment with different wine pairings, consider trying a dry white wine like Chardonnay or Sauvignon Blanc. These crisp, refreshing wines provide a perfect contrast to the salty, briny flavor of the caviar, creating a dynamic flavor profile that will tantalize your taste buds.

For those who prefer red wine, a light-bodied Pinot Noir or Merlot can also make an excellent pairing with caviar. The subtle notes of fruit and earthiness in these wines complement the delicate flavor of the caviar without overpowering it, creating a well-balanced pairing that is sure to impress even the most discerning palate.

No matter which pairing you choose, the key is to experiment and find the combination that works best for your own unique taste preferences. Whether you prefer the classic pairing of champagne and caviar or want to try something new with a different type of wine, the art of caviar pairing is all about finding the perfect balance of flavors to create a truly unforgettable dining experience. Cheers to the perfect pairing!

Caviar Tasting Notes

Caviar tasting notes are an essential part of the caviar connoisseur's experience. The unique flavors, textures, and aromas of different types of caviar can vary greatly, making each tasting session a truly special and memorable occasion. When paired with the right champagne or wine, the flavors of caviar can be elevated to new heights, creating a truly indulgent and luxurious experience for the palate.

One of the most important aspects of caviar tasting notes is the distinction between different types of caviar. From the delicate and buttery flavor of Osetra caviar to the briny and bold taste of Beluga caviar, each variety offers a distinct sensory experience that can be enhanced through careful pairing with the right champagne or wine. By paying attention to the nuances of each type of caviar, connoisseurs can better appreciate the complexity and depth of flavor that these luxurious delicacies have to offer.

When tasting caviar, it is important to pay attention to the texture of the eggs, as well as the intensity of the flavor. The size, shape, and color of the eggs can also provide valuable information about the quality and freshness of the caviar. By taking the time to carefully observe and assess these characteristics, caviar connoisseurs can develop a more nuanced understanding of the subtle differences between different types of caviar, allowing them to better appreciate the unique qualities of each variety.

In addition to paying attention to the taste and texture of the caviar itself, connoisseurs should also consider the impact of the champagne or wine they choose to pair with it. The right pairing can enhance the flavors of the caviar, creating a harmonious balance that allows each element to shine. Whether opting for a crisp and refreshing champagne to complement the briny notes of Osetra caviar or a rich and full-bodied red wine to enhance the creaminess of Beluga caviar, the possibilities for caviar pairing are endless.

In conclusion, caviar tasting notes offer a wealth of information for caviar connoisseurs looking to enhance their appreciation of these luxurious delicacies. By paying attention to the unique flavors, textures, and aromas of different types of caviar, connoisseurs can develop a more nuanced understanding of the complexities of this indulgent treat. When paired with the right champagne or wine, caviar tasting notes can help connoisseurs create truly memorable and enjoyable tasting experiences that celebrate the exquisite flavors of these prized delicacies.

Chapter 7: Exploring New Caviar and Wine Pairings

Experimental Pairings

For the adventurous caviar connoisseur, the world of experimental pairings opens up a whole new realm of possibilities. While traditional pairings of caviar with champagne and wine are undeniably classic and delicious, there is something truly exciting about pushing the boundaries and exploring unexpected flavor combinations.

One such experimental pairing that has been gaining popularity in recent years is caviar paired with sake. The subtle sweetness and umami flavors of sake complement the briny, buttery notes of caviar in a truly unique way. Try pairing a high-quality ossetra caviar with a smooth, slightly sweet Junmai sake for a pairing that is sure to delight your taste buds.

Another unconventional pairing to consider is caviar with craft beer. The effervescence and complex flavors of craft beer can provide a surprising contrast to the rich, luxurious taste of caviar. For a fun and unexpected pairing, try pairing a creamy sturgeon caviar with a hoppy IPA or a crisp pilsner.

For those looking to elevate their caviar pairing experience even further, consider experimenting with pairing caviar with a fine single malt whisky. The smoky, peaty flavors of a good Scotch whisky can create a beautiful harmony with the salty, briny notes of caviar. Opt for a delicate, buttery caviar like beluga and pair it with a rich, full-bodied Scotch for a truly decadent experience.

While experimenting with unconventional pairings can be a fun and rewarding experience, it is important to remember that the key to successful caviar pairing lies in balance. The flavors of the caviar, champagne, wine, or other beverage should complement each other, creating a harmonious and enjoyable tasting experience. So go ahead, get creative, and don't be afraid to try something new – you never know what delicious discoveries you might make in the world of experimental pairings.

Regional Pairings

For caviar connoisseurs looking to elevate their tasting experience, understanding regional pairings is essential. Different types of caviar from various regions around the world have unique flavor profiles that can be enhanced or complemented by specific champagnes and wines. By exploring regional pairings, you can create a harmonious balance of flavors that will tantalize your taste buds and leave you craving more.

One classic regional pairing that never fails to impress is Russian Ossetra caviar with a crisp, dry Champagne. The buttery texture and nutty flavor of the caviar pairs perfectly with the effervescence and acidity of the Champagne, creating a luxurious and decadent tasting experience. The subtle sweetness of the Champagne helps to balance out the saltiness of the caviar, creating a perfect harmony of flavors on the palate.

For those looking to explore a more unique regional pairing, Iranian Beluga caviar with a full-bodied red wine from Bordeaux is a match made in heaven. The rich, creamy texture of the caviar is beautifully complemented by the bold tannins and fruity notes of the Bordeaux wine, creating a complex and indulgent flavor profile that will leave you speechless. This pairing is perfect for those looking to indulge in a truly decadent tasting experience.

If you're a fan of American caviar, pairing California White Sturgeon caviar with a crisp, dry Sauvignon Blanc is a winning combination. The clean, briny flavors of the caviar are enhanced by the bright acidity and citrus notes of the Sauvignon Blanc, creating a refreshing and palate-cleansing pairing that is perfect for a light and elegant tasting experience. This regional pairing is ideal for those looking for a more modern and innovative approach to caviar pairing.

For a truly decadent and indulgent tasting experience, pairing French Oscietra caviar with a rich and buttery Chardonnay from Burgundy is a must-try. The creamy texture and nutty flavor of the caviar are beautifully complemented by the oak-aged notes and buttery finish of the Chardonnay, creating a luxurious and sophisticated pairing that is sure to impress even the most discerning caviar connoisseur. This regional pairing is perfect for those looking to indulge in a truly decadent and unforgettable tasting experience.

In conclusion, exploring regional pairings is a fantastic way to enhance your caviar tasting experience and discover new and exciting flavor combinations. Whether you prefer Russian, Iranian, American, or French caviar, there is a perfect champagne or wine pairing waiting for you to discover. So grab a bottle of your favorite champagne or wine, select your caviar of choice, and embark on a culinary journey that will tantalize your taste buds and leave you craving more. Cheers to the art of caviar pairing!

Customizing Your Pairings

As a caviar connoisseur, one of the most exciting aspects of enjoying this luxurious delicacy is the opportunity to customize your pairings with different champagnes and wines. By experimenting with various flavor profiles, textures, and aromas, you can elevate your caviar tasting experience to new heights. In this subchapter, we will explore the art of customizing your pairings to create unforgettable culinary combinations that will delight your senses and enhance the flavors of both the caviar and the beverages.

When it comes to pairing caviar with champagne, it's essential to consider the characteristics of both the caviar and the bubbly. For example, a light and delicate caviar such as Osetra or Sevruga pairs beautifully with a crisp and refreshing Blanc de Blancs champagne, which complements the subtle flavors of the caviar without overpowering them. On the other hand, a rich and buttery caviar like Beluga or Imperial can stand up to a more full-bodied champagne like a Vintage Brut or a Rosé, which adds depth and complexity to the pairing.

Similarly, when pairing caviar with wine, it's important to match the flavors and textures of the caviar with the characteristics of the wine. For example, a creamy and nutty caviar like Siberian or Kaluga pairs well with a Chardonnay or a Pinot Gris, which have a buttery richness that enhances the caviar's flavors. On the other hand, a briny and savory caviar like Sevruga or Sterlet is best paired with a crisp and acidic Sauvignon Blanc or a Riesling, which help to balance out the saltiness of the caviar and cleanse the palate between bites.

To truly customize your pairings, consider experimenting with different combinations of caviar, champagne, and wine to discover your own unique preferences. Whether you prefer a classic pairing like Beluga caviar with a Vintage Brut champagne or a more unconventional pairing like Osetra caviar with a Pinot Noir wine, the possibilities are endless. By taking the time to explore and experiment with different flavor profiles, textures, and aromas, you can create personalized pairings that reflect your individual taste and enhance your caviar tasting experience.

In conclusion, the art of customizing your pairings is a fun and rewarding way to enhance your caviar tasting experience and create unforgettable culinary combinations. By considering the characteristics of both the caviar and the beverages, experimenting with different combinations, and following your own preferences, you can create personalized pairings that elevate the flavors of both the caviar and the champagne or wine. Whether you prefer a classic pairing or a more unconventional combination, the key is to have fun, be creative, and savor every bite and sip. Cheers to the art of caviar pairing!

Chapter 8: Conclusion and Resources

Final Thoughts

In conclusion, mastering the art of caviar pairing with champagne and wines is truly a journey worth embarking on for any caviar connoisseur. The intricate dance of flavors that unfolds on your palate as you carefully select the perfect pairing is a true testament to the sophistication and elegance of this culinary experience. With the right guidance and knowledge, you can elevate your caviar tasting to a whole new level of enjoyment.

As you continue to explore the world of caviar pairing, remember to trust your instincts and experiment with different combinations. The beauty of this art lies in its subjectivity, as what may work for one palate may not necessarily work for another. Don't be afraid to push the boundaries and try unconventional pairings – you never know what hidden gems you may discover.

It is also important to pay attention to the quality of both the caviar and the champagne or wine you are pairing it with. Opt for the highest quality ingredients you can afford, as this will truly make a difference in the overall experience. Seek out expert advice from sommeliers and caviar experts to help guide you in making informed choices.

Above all, remember to savor each bite and sip, allowing yourself to fully immerse in the sensory experience that caviar pairing offers. Take the time to appreciate the nuances of flavors and textures, and relish in the luxury of indulging in such a decadent treat. Whether you are hosting a lavish soirée or simply treating yourself to a special meal, caviar pairing with champagne and wines is an experience that is sure to leave a lasting impression.

In the end, the art of caviar pairing is a true celebration of the finer things in life. It is a testament to the craftsmanship and dedication that goes into creating these exquisite delicacies, and a tribute to the timeless tradition of enjoying the finer things in life. So raise your glass, savor the taste of the sea, and toast to the exquisite pairing of caviar with champagne and wines – a culinary experience like no other. Cheers!

Additional Reading and Resources

For those who are truly passionate about caviar pairing with champagne and wines, there are always more resources and reading materials to explore. Whether you are a seasoned caviar connoisseur or just starting to delve into the world of luxury pairings, there is always more to learn and discover. In this subchapter, we will introduce some additional reading and resources that can help deepen your knowledge and appreciation of caviar and its perfect pairings.

One of the must-read books for caviar connoisseurs is "Caviar: A Global History" by Nichola Fletcher. This book provides a comprehensive overview of the history, production, and cultural significance of caviar. It delves into the different types of caviar, the best ways to enjoy it, and the traditions surrounding this delicacy. It is a fascinating read that will enhance your understanding of caviar and its place in the culinary world.

If you are looking for more specific guidance on pairing caviar with champagne and wines, "The Champagne Guide" by Tyson Stelzer is a valuable resource. Stelzer is a renowned wine critic and champagne expert, and his book offers detailed insights into the world of champagne. From the best champagne houses to the perfect pairings with caviar, this book is a must-have for anyone interested in the art of caviar pairing.

For those who prefer a more interactive approach to learning, there are also plenty of online resources available. Websites such as Caviar Star and Caviar Lover offer in-depth guides on caviar types, tasting notes, and pairing suggestions. These websites are a great way to expand your knowledge and discover new caviar and champagne combinations to try.

In addition to books and online resources, attending caviar and champagne tasting events can be a fantastic way to further your expertise. These events often feature expert sommeliers and chefs who can provide valuable insights and recommendations. Keep an eye out for upcoming events in your area or consider organizing your own tasting party with friends to explore different pairings and find your favorites.

In conclusion, the world of caviar pairing with champagne and wines is a rich and exciting one, with endless opportunities for exploration and discovery. By delving into additional reading and resources, you can enhance your knowledge and appreciation of this luxurious culinary art. Whether you prefer to learn from books, websites, or hands-on experiences, there are plenty of resources available to help you become a true caviar connoisseur.

Glossary of Terms

In the world of caviar pairing with champagne and wines, it is essential to have a good understanding of the terminology used in this niche. This glossary of terms is designed to help caviar connoisseurs navigate the complexities of pairing caviar with their favorite beverages.

1. Caviar: Caviar refers to the salt-cured eggs of sturgeon fish, which are considered a delicacy around the world. There are different types of caviar, including Beluga, Osetra, and Sevruga, each with its own unique flavor profile and texture.

2. Champagne: Champagne is a sparkling wine produced in the Champagne region of France. It is known for its effervescence, acidity, and complex flavor profile, making it an ideal pairing for caviar. The bubbles in champagne help cleanse the palate between bites of caviar, enhancing the overall tasting experience.

3. Wine: Wine is a fermented beverage made from grapes that can be produced in various styles, including red, white, and rosé. When pairing wine with caviar, it is essential to consider the acidity, tannins, and fruitiness of the wine to complement the flavors of the caviar.

4. Brut: Brut is a term used to describe dry champagne or sparkling wine with minimal residual sugar. Brut wines are popular choices for pairing with caviar because their crisp acidity and effervescence help cut through the richness of the caviar, creating a harmonious balance of flavors.

5. Terroir: Terroir refers to the unique environmental factors, such as soil, climate, and topography, that influence the flavor and character of grapes used to make wine. Understanding terroir is essential for caviar connoisseurs looking to create the perfect pairing with champagne and wine, as it can help enhance the overall tasting experience by highlighting the complementary flavors of both the caviar and the beverage.

Chapter heading page

Eating caviar is an experience that transcends the mere act of consumption; it is a ritual steeped in centuries of tradition and elegance. From the delicate texture of the eggs to the burst of briny flavor on the palate, every aspect of enjoying caviar has been refined to enhance its unique qualities. One crucial aspect often overlooked is the choice of utensils, particularly the importance of avoiding metal spoons. The reasons for this are rooted in both the sensory impact on the caviar and the historical traditions that surround its consumption.

Sensory Impact: The Delicate Nature of Caviar

Caviar, the salted roe of sturgeon, is highly sensitive to its environment. This sensitivity extends to the utensils used to serve and eat it. Metal spoons, commonly made from materials like stainless steel or silver, can adversely affect the delicate balance of flavors in caviar.

Oxidation and Metallic Taste

When caviar comes into contact with metal, a chemical reaction can occur, leading to oxidation. This process can impart a metallic taste to the caviar, overshadowing its natural, nuanced flavors. The slight saltiness, the buttery notes, and the oceanic undertones can be masked by an unpleasant metallic tang, diminishing the overall experience. The purity of caviar's flavor is one of its most prized attributes, and using a metal spoon risks compromising this purity.

Texture and Temperature

Caviar's texture is as important as its flavor. The eggs should be firm, yet delicate enough to burst lightly in the mouth. Metal spoons, depending on their temperature, can alter the texture of the caviar. A cold metal spoon can slightly harden the eggs, while a warm spoon can cause them to soften too much. In either case, the ideal consistency of the caviar is compromised, leading to a less enjoyable experience.

Tradition and Aesthetics: The Cultural Significance

The traditions surrounding caviar consumption are as rich and storied as the delicacy itself. Historically, caviar has been a symbol of luxury and opulence, often enjoyed by royalty and the elite. The utensils used in its consumption have evolved to reflect this status, with a focus on preserving the integrity of the caviar.

Non-Metal Alternatives

Traditionally, non-metal spoons made from materials like mother of pearl, bone, horn, or even gold have been used to serve caviar. Each of these materials has been chosen for specific reasons related to both functionality and tradition.

- **Mother of Pearl**: Perhaps the most iconic material for caviar spoons, mother of pearl is non-reactive, ensuring that the caviar's flavor remains untainted. Its smooth, lustrous surface also complements the visual appeal of the caviar, enhancing the overall aesthetic of the presentation.

- **Bone and Horn**: These materials, often used historically, are also non-reactive and provide a rustic yet elegant touch to the caviar experience. They are particularly favored in traditional Russian caviar service.

- **Gold**: As a noble metal, gold does not react with the caviar, preserving its taste. Gold spoons add a layer of opulence to the caviar service, aligning with the luxurious nature of the delicacy.

Historical Context

The use of non-metal spoons dates back to times when caviar was a staple at the tables of Russian tsars and Persian shahs. These cultures placed a high value on the purity and presentation of caviar, leading to the development of specialized utensils that would not interfere with the delicate flavors of the roe. This historical precedent underscores the importance of using the right utensils to fully appreciate caviar.

Practical Considerations: Enhancing the Caviar Experience

Beyond tradition and sensory impact, practical considerations also play a role in the choice of utensils for caviar consumption. Ensuring that the caviar retains its optimal flavor and texture can significantly enhance the overall experience.

Cost and Investment

Caviar is a luxury item, often accompanied by a significant price tag. Given the investment involved in procuring high-quality caviar, it makes sense to take every measure to ensure that it is enjoyed to its fullest potential. Using a metal spoon, which can detract from the flavor, is counterproductive to this goal. Investing in a proper caviar spoon, made from non-reactive materials, is a small but meaningful step toward preserving the quality of the caviar.

Ritual and Appreciation

The act of eating caviar is more than just consuming food; it is a ritual that invites appreciation and mindfulness. From the way it is served to the utensils used, every detail contributes to the overall experience. Using a non-metal spoon is part of this ritual, signaling a respect for the traditions and nuances that make caviar special. It elevates the act of eating caviar from a simple meal to a ceremonious event.

Conclusion: Respecting the Delicacy

In conclusion, the reasons for avoiding metal spoons when eating caviar are multifaceted, encompassing sensory, traditional, and practical considerations. The delicate nature of caviar, with its sensitivity to oxidation and temperature, demands the use of non-reactive utensils to preserve its pristine flavor and texture. The historical and cultural significance of non-metal spoons underscores the importance of maintaining traditions that honor the luxurious nature of caviar. Furthermore, the investment in high-quality caviar deserves the best possible experience, which includes the thoughtful choice of utensils.

Ultimately, the use of a non-metal spoon is a simple yet profound gesture that demonstrates an understanding and respect for the delicacy of caviar. It ensures that every bite is savored in its purest form, allowing the true essence of this extraordinary food to shine through. By adhering to this tradition, we honor the centuries of refinement that have made caviar one of the most cherished and luxurious foods in the world.

The Health Benefits of Eating Fine Caviar

Caviar, the salted roe of sturgeon, has long been associated with luxury and indulgence. While its rich history and high status in culinary circles are well known, its health benefits are often overlooked. Caviar is not only a gourmet delicacy but also a nutrient-dense food that offers numerous health advantages. This comprehensive exploration delves into the various health benefits of eating fine caviar, supported by scientific evidence and nutritional analysis.

Nutritional Profile of Caviar

Before delving into the specific health benefits, it is essential to understand the nutritional composition of caviar. Caviar is rich in several essential nutrients, making it a valuable addition to a balanced diet. Key components of caviar include:

- **Proteins**: Caviar is an excellent source of high-quality protein, containing all essential amino acids necessary for the body's functions.

- **Fats**: While caviar is high in fat, it primarily consists of healthy omega-3 fatty acids, which are beneficial for heart health.

- **Vitamins**: Caviar is rich in vitamins A, D, E, and B12, which play crucial roles in various bodily functions, including immune support, bone health, and energy metabolism.

- **Minerals**: It contains essential minerals such as calcium, phosphorus, selenium, magnesium, and iron, which are vital for bone health, energy production, and maintaining healthy red blood cells.

- **Antioxidants**: The presence of antioxidants in caviar helps protect cells from oxidative stress and may reduce the risk of chronic diseases.

Cardiovascular Health

One of the most significant health benefits of eating caviar is its positive impact on cardiovascular health. This benefit is primarily due to the high content of omega-3 fatty acids, specifically eicosapentaenoic acid (EPA) and docosahexaenoic acid (DHA).

Omega-3 Fatty Acids and Heart Health

Omega-3 fatty acids are well-known for their cardioprotective properties. Regular consumption of these fatty acids has been associated with several heart health benefits, including:

- **Reduced Risk of Heart Disease**: Studies have shown that omega-3 fatty acids can help lower triglyceride levels, reduce inflammation, and improve overall heart health, thereby decreasing the risk of heart disease.

- **Lower Blood Pressure**: Omega-3 fatty acids have been found to help lower blood pressure in individuals with hypertension, reducing the strain on the cardiovascular system.

- **Improved Cholesterol Levels**: Consuming omega-3s can increase levels of high-density lipoprotein (HDL) cholesterol, known as the "good" cholesterol, and decrease levels of low-density lipoprotein (LDL) cholesterol, the "bad" cholesterol.

- **Prevention of Arrhythmias**: Omega-3s can help prevent irregular heartbeats (arrhythmias), which can lead to sudden cardiac death.

Antioxidant Properties

Caviar contains antioxidants, such as vitamin E and selenium, which play a crucial role in protecting the cardiovascular system. These antioxidants help neutralize free radicals, reducing oxidative stress and preventing damage to the heart and blood vessels.

Brain Health

Caviar is also beneficial for brain health, thanks to its rich content of omega-3 fatty acids, particularly DHA. DHA is a critical component of brain cell membranes and is essential for proper brain function.

Cognitive Function and Mental Health

Regular consumption of DHA has been linked to several cognitive benefits, including:

- **Improved Cognitive Function**: DHA is essential for maintaining cognitive function and preventing cognitive decline. Studies have shown that higher levels of DHA are associated with better memory, learning, and overall cognitive performance.

- **Reduced Risk of Alzheimer's Disease**: Some research suggests that adequate intake of DHA may reduce the risk of Alzheimer's disease and other forms of dementia by preventing the buildup of amyloid plaques in the brain.

- **Mental Health Benefits**: Omega-3 fatty acids, including DHA, have been shown to have mood-stabilizing effects and may help reduce symptoms of depression and anxiety. They play a role in regulating neurotransmitters and reducing inflammation in the brain, which are linked to mood disorders.

Eye Health

DHA is not only crucial for brain health but also for maintaining good vision. It is a major component of the retina, and adequate levels of DHA are necessary for optimal eye function.

Prevention of Age-Related Macular Degeneration

Age-related macular degeneration (AMD) is a common eye condition that can lead to vision loss in older adults. Studies have shown that omega-3 fatty acids, particularly DHA, may help prevent or slow the progression of AMD by protecting the retina from oxidative damage and inflammation.

Improvement in Dry Eye Syndrome

Dry eye syndrome is a condition where the eyes do not produce enough tears, leading to discomfort and potential vision problems. Omega-3 fatty acids can help improve tear production and reduce the symptoms of dry eye syndrome, providing relief for affected individuals.

Bone Health

Caviar is rich in several nutrients that are essential for maintaining healthy bones, including vitamin D, calcium, phosphorus, and magnesium.

Vitamin D and Calcium Absorption

Vitamin D plays a crucial role in calcium absorption, which is necessary for maintaining strong bones. Adequate levels of vitamin D help ensure that calcium from the diet is effectively absorbed and utilized by the body, reducing the risk of osteoporosis and fractures.

Phosphorus and Bone Strength

Phosphorus is another essential mineral found in caviar that contributes to bone health. It works in conjunction with calcium to build and maintain strong bones and teeth. Adequate phosphorus intake is necessary for proper bone mineralization and overall skeletal health.

Immune System Support

Caviar contains several nutrients that support the immune system, including vitamins A, C, and E, as well as selenium and zinc.

Vitamin A

Vitamin A is crucial for maintaining the health of the immune system. It helps regulate the production and function of white blood cells, which are essential for fighting off infections and diseases. Adequate vitamin A levels can enhance the body's ability to defend against pathogens and maintain overall immune function.

Selenium and Zinc

Selenium and zinc are essential minerals that play vital roles in immune function. Selenium acts as an antioxidant, protecting cells from damage and supporting the immune response. Zinc is necessary for the development and function of immune cells, and it helps maintain the integrity of the skin and mucous membranes, which act as barriers against infections.

Skin Health

The nutrients found in caviar, including omega-3 fatty acids, vitamins A and E, and antioxidants, contribute to healthy and radiant skin.

Omega-3 Fatty Acids and Skin Hydration

Omega-3 fatty acids help maintain the skin's lipid barrier, which is essential for retaining moisture and preventing dryness. Adequate intake of omega-3s can improve skin hydration, reduce inflammation, and promote a healthy complexion.

Vitamin E and Antioxidant Protection

Vitamin E is a powerful antioxidant that protects the skin from oxidative damage caused by free radicals. It helps reduce the signs of aging, such as wrinkles and fine lines, by neutralizing free radicals and promoting skin repair.

Anti-Inflammatory Benefits

Chronic inflammation is a common underlying factor in many chronic diseases, including heart disease, diabetes, and autoimmune disorders. The anti-inflammatory properties of caviar's omega-3 fatty acids can help reduce inflammation and lower the risk of developing these conditions.

Reduction of Inflammatory Markers

Omega-3 fatty acids have been shown to reduce levels of inflammatory markers, such as C-reactive protein (CRP) and interleukin-6 (IL-6). By lowering these markers, caviar can help mitigate the inflammatory response and promote overall health.

Muscle and Joint Health

The high protein content in caviar, along with its anti-inflammatory properties, makes it beneficial for muscle and joint health.

Protein for Muscle Repair and Growth

Protein is essential for muscle repair and growth. The amino acids in caviar provide the building blocks necessary for maintaining and repairing muscle tissue. Regular consumption of caviar can support muscle recovery after exercise and promote overall muscle health.

Omega-3s and Joint Health

The anti-inflammatory effects of omega-3 fatty acids can help reduce joint inflammation and alleviate symptoms of conditions such as arthritis. Omega-3s may help improve joint mobility and reduce pain, enhancing the quality of life for individuals with joint issues.

Reproductive Health

Caviar is rich in several nutrients that support reproductive health, including omega-3 fatty acids, vitamins, and minerals.

Omega-3s and Fertility

Omega-3 fatty acids play a role in reproductive health by regulating hormone levels and supporting the health of reproductive tissues. In women, omega-3s can help regulate menstrual cycles and improve egg quality. In men, omega-3s can enhance sperm quality and motility.

Vitamins and Minerals for Reproductive Health

Vitamins A, D, and E, as well as minerals such as zinc and selenium, are essential for reproductive health. These nutrients support the development and function of reproductive organs, promote healthy hormone levels, and protect reproductive cells from oxidative damage.

Weight Management

While caviar is a calorie-dense food, its high protein and healthy fat content can support weight management efforts.

Satiety and Appetite Control

The protein and fat in caviar can promote feelings of satiety and help control appetite. Including caviar in meals can reduce overall calorie intake by making you feel fuller for longer, thereby supporting weight management goals.

Conclusion

The health benefits of eating fine caviar are numerous and well-supported by scientific evidence. Its rich nutritional profile, including high-quality proteins, healthy fats, essential vitamins and minerals, and antioxidants, makes it a valuable addition to a balanced diet. From promoting cardiovascular and brain health to supporting immune function and skin health, the benefits of caviar extend far beyond its luxurious reputation. Including caviar in your diet can provide a host of health advantages, making it

The World of Fine Caviar: Types, Prices, and What Makes Them Special

Caviar, the salted roe of sturgeon, has been a symbol of luxury and gourmet indulgence for centuries. Each type of caviar carries its own unique characteristics, flavors, and textures, contributing to its allure and value. This comprehensive exploration delves into the different types of fine caviar, highlighting what makes each variety special, and examining the factors that contribute to their varying prices, including the most expensive caviars in the world.

The Basics of Caviar

Caviar comes from various species of sturgeon, each producing eggs with distinct qualities. The primary species include Beluga, Osetra, and Sevruga, but there are several other types worth noting. The caviar's flavor, texture, color, and size vary significantly depending on the species of sturgeon and the conditions in which it is raised.

Types of Caviar by Sturgeon Species

1. **Beluga (Huso huso)**

2. **Osetra (Acipenser gueldenstaedtii)**

3. **Sevruga (Acipenser stellatus)**

4. **Kaluga (Huso dauricus)**

5. **Sterlet (Acipenser ruthenus)**

6. **Siberian Sturgeon (Acipenser baerii)**

7. **American Sturgeon (Acipenser fulvescens)**

Beluga Caviar

Characteristics

Beluga caviar is often considered the pinnacle of luxury. It is derived from the Beluga sturgeon, the largest of the sturgeon species, which can live for over a century and take up to 20 years to mature. The eggs are the largest among caviars, often ranging from pea-sized to larger.

- **Flavor**: Delicate, buttery, and creamy with a slightly nutty undertone.

- **Texture**: Soft and smooth, with a melt-in-the-mouth consistency.

- **Color**: Varies from light to dark gray, with the lightest and largest eggs being the most prized.

Price and Rarity

Beluga caviar is the most expensive caviar available due to several factors:

- **Scarcity**: The Beluga sturgeon is critically endangered, and strict regulations limit its harvest.

- **Maturity Time**: The long maturation period (up to 20 years) adds to the cost.

- **Size and Flavor**: The large, delicate eggs and unparalleled flavor profile command a premium price.

Top Varieties

- **Almas Caviar**: This rare variety of Beluga caviar comes from albino sturgeons. It is prized for its golden color and exquisite flavor, often fetching prices upwards of $25,000 per kilogram, making it the most expensive caviar in the world.

Osetra Caviar

Characteristics

Osetra caviar comes from the Osetra sturgeon, which matures faster than the Beluga (around 12-15 years). Osetra is highly regarded for its rich and complex flavor.

- **Flavor**: Nutty and briny with a rich, creamy texture.

- **Texture**: Firm and smooth, with a pleasing pop when eaten.

- **Color**: Varies from golden yellow to dark brown.

Price and Popularity

Osetra caviar is one of the most popular and widely consumed types of caviar. It is generally less expensive than Beluga but still commands a high price due to its superior quality and flavor.

- **Golden Osetra**: The rarest and most expensive variety of Osetra caviar, known for its golden hue and exceptional taste, can cost over $10,000 per kilogram.

Sevruga Caviar

Characteristics

Sevruga caviar is derived from the Sevruga sturgeon, which matures faster than both Beluga and Osetra (around 7-10 years). It is known for its small, delicate eggs.

- **Flavor**: Strong, pronounced, and slightly salty, with a briny finish.

- **Texture**: Firm yet delicate, with a noticeable pop.

- **Color**: Light to dark gray.

Price and Accessibility

Sevruga caviar is generally more accessible and less expensive than Beluga and Osetra due to the shorter maturation period and higher availability. However, it is still considered a premium product.

- **Classic Sevruga**: This variety is well-regarded for its consistent quality and flavor, typically priced around $3,000 to $5,000 per kilogram.

Kaluga Caviar

Characteristics

Kaluga caviar is often compared to Beluga caviar due to its similar size and flavor profile. It comes from the Kaluga sturgeon, which is native to the Amur River basin in China and Russia.

- **Flavor**: Rich, creamy, and buttery, similar to Beluga but slightly more briny.

- **Texture**: Large, firm eggs with a smooth, luxurious texture.

- **Color**: Light to dark brown.

Price and Market

Kaluga caviar is prized for its quality and is often considered an excellent alternative to Beluga. Prices range from $5,000 to $8,000 per kilogram, depending on the quality and size of the eggs.

Sterlet Caviar

Characteristics

Sterlet caviar comes from the Sterlet sturgeon, a smaller species that produces small, delicate eggs. It is less common but highly valued for its unique flavor.

- **Flavor**: Mild, slightly sweet, and delicate with a clean finish.

- **Texture**: Fine and smooth, with a soft texture.

- **Color**: Light gray to gold.

Price and Availability

Sterlet caviar is less widely available and can be more expensive due to its rarity. Prices typically range from $4,000 to $6,000 per kilogram.

Siberian Sturgeon Caviar

Characteristics

Siberian sturgeon caviar, derived from the Siberian sturgeon, is known for its distinct flavor and medium-sized eggs. The sturgeon matures relatively quickly (around 6-8 years).

- **Flavor**: Earthy and briny with a hint of sweetness.

- **Texture**: Medium-firm eggs with a pleasant pop.

- **Color**: Dark gray to black.

Price and Popularity

Siberian sturgeon caviar is popular due to its affordability and quality. Prices typically range from $1,500 to $3,000 per kilogram, making it a more accessible option for caviar enthusiasts.

American Sturgeon Caviar

Characteristics

American sturgeon caviar comes from several species native to North America, including the White sturgeon and Paddlefish. It is known for its high quality and unique flavor profile.

- **Flavor**: Mild, earthy, and slightly nutty with a clean finish.

- **Texture**: Medium-firm eggs with a smooth texture.

- **Color**: Light to dark gray.

Price and Market

American sturgeon caviar is gaining popularity due to sustainable farming practices and high quality. Prices range from $1,000 to $2,500 per kilogram.

Factors Influencing Caviar Prices

Several factors contribute to the varying prices of caviar, including the type of sturgeon, the caviar's quality, and the production methods.

Species and Rarity

- **Species**: Different sturgeon species produce caviar with varying qualities and flavors, affecting the price. Beluga caviar, for instance, is the most expensive due to its superior quality and rarity.

- **Rarity**: Caviar from endangered species or those with limited availability, like the Beluga and Sterlet, commands higher prices.

Maturation Time

- **Maturation Time**: Sturgeon that take longer to mature, such as Beluga and Osetra, result in higher caviar prices due to the extended time and resources required for production.

Quality and Grading

- **Grading**: Caviar is graded based on the size, color, texture, and flavor of the eggs. Higher-grade caviar, with larger, more uniform eggs and superior flavor, is more expensive.

- **Quality**: The quality of the caviar, including the freshness and handling during production, significantly impacts the price.

Farming and Sustainability

- **Farming Practices**: Sustainable and ethical farming practices can affect the price of caviar. Wild-caught caviar is often more expensive due to the challenges and regulations associated with harvesting from wild sturgeon populations.

- **Sustainability**: Caviar from farms that prioritize sustainability and conservation efforts may command higher prices due to the added costs of maintaining ethical practices.

Conclusion

The world of fine caviar is diverse and complex, with each type offering unique flavors, textures, and experiences. From the opulent Beluga and its rare Almas variety to the more accessible but equally delightful Siberian and American sturgeon caviars, there is a type of caviar to suit every palate and occasion. The prices of caviar are influenced by various factors, including the species of sturgeon, the quality and grading of the eggs, and the farming practices employed. By understanding these factors and the distinctive characteristics of each type of caviar, enthusiasts can better appreciate the nuances and luxury that this exquisite delicacy offers.

The Proper Way to Serve Fine Caviar: Dishes, Etiquette, and Presentation

Caviar, with its rich heritage and luxurious appeal, is not merely a delicacy; it is an experience that requires careful attention to detail. The proper way to serve fine caviar encompasses a variety of factors, including the choice of utensils, accompaniments, presentation, and etiquette. This comprehensive guide delves into the best practices for serving caviar, ensuring that it is enjoyed to its fullest potential.

The Basics of Serving Caviar

Storing Caviar

Proper storage of caviar is crucial to maintaining its quality and flavor. Here are the key points to consider:

- **Temperature**: Caviar should be stored at temperatures between 28°F and 32°F (-2°C to 0°C). The coldest part of the refrigerator, usually the back or the bottom shelf, is ideal.

- **Airtight Containers**: Caviar should be kept in its original airtight tin or jar to prevent exposure to air, which can lead to oxidation and spoilage.

- **Short-Term Storage**: Once opened, caviar should be consumed within 1-2 days to ensure freshness. Unopened caviar can typically be stored for up to four weeks in the refrigerator.

- **Avoid Freezing**: Freezing caviar is not recommended as it can alter the texture and flavor of the eggs.

Choosing the Right Utensils

The utensils used to serve and eat caviar play a significant role in preserving its delicate flavor:

- **Non-Metallic Spoons**: Metal spoons can impart a metallic taste to the caviar. Instead, use spoons made from non-reactive materials such as mother of pearl, bone, horn, or gold.

- **Caviar Server**: A caviar server, often made of crystal or glass, can be used to present the caviar elegantly. It usually includes a bowl for ice to keep the caviar chilled.

Presentation

The presentation of caviar is an art form that enhances the dining experience:

- **Ice Bed**: Place the caviar tin or jar on a bed of crushed ice to keep it chilled throughout the serving. This not only maintains the ideal temperature but also adds a touch of elegance.

- **Garnishes**: Fresh herbs like dill or chives can be used as garnishes to add color and complement the caviar's flavor.

- **Minimal Handling**: Handle the caviar as little as possible to avoid crushing the delicate eggs. Use a gentle hand when transferring caviar from its container to the serving dish.

Traditional Accompaniments

Traditional accompaniments enhance the caviar experience by providing complementary flavors and textures. Here are some classic options:

Blini

Blini, small Russian pancakes, are a traditional accompaniment to caviar. They are soft and slightly sweet, providing a neutral base that allows the caviar's flavors to shine.

- **Preparation**: Blini are typically made from a batter of buckwheat or wheat flour, milk, eggs, and yeast. They are cooked on a griddle until golden brown.

- **Serving**: Serve warm blini with a dollop of crème fraîche and a spoonful of caviar on top. The combination of the warm blini, creamy crème fraîche, and briny caviar creates a harmonious bite.

Crème Fraîche

Crème fraîche, a tangy and creamy cultured cream, is a perfect match for caviar. Its rich texture balances the brininess of the caviar.

- **Serving**: Serve crème fraîche in a small bowl alongside the caviar. It can be spread on blini, toast points, or crackers before adding the caviar.

Toast Points and Crackers

Toast points and crackers provide a crisp and sturdy base for caviar:

- **Toast Points**: Cut slices of white or brioche bread into small triangles and toast until golden and crisp.

- **Crackers**: Choose plain, unsalted crackers to avoid overpowering the caviar's delicate flavor.

Hard-Boiled Eggs

Hard-boiled eggs, both the whites and the yolks, can be finely chopped and served with caviar. The mild flavor and creamy texture of the eggs complement the caviar without overshadowing it.

Onions and Chives

Finely diced red onions or chopped chives add a subtle bite and freshness to the caviar experience. Serve them in small bowls for guests to sprinkle on their caviar as desired.

Lemon Wedges

Lemon wedges can be provided for those who enjoy a touch of acidity with their caviar. A light squeeze of lemon can enhance the caviar's natural flavors.

Creative Serving Ideas

While traditional accompaniments are always a safe choice, creative serving ideas can elevate the caviar experience:

Caviar Canapés

Canapés are small, bite-sized appetizers that can be topped with caviar:

- **Cucumber Rounds**: Slice cucumbers into rounds and top with a dollop of crème fraîche and a spoonful of caviar.

- **Potato Chips**: High-quality, plain potato chips can provide a delightful crunch to contrast with the soft caviar.

- **Endive Leaves**: Use endive leaves as a natural vessel for caviar, crème fraîche, and garnishes.

Sushi and Sashimi

Caviar can add a luxurious touch to sushi and sashimi:

- **Nigiri**: Place a small spoonful of caviar on top of nigiri sushi for an elegant presentation.

- **Sashimi**: Add a spoonful of caviar to slices of sashimi for a burst of flavor and texture.

Deviled Eggs

Deviled eggs can be enhanced with caviar:

- **Classic Deviled Eggs**: Prepare deviled eggs with a creamy filling and top each half with a small spoonful of caviar.

- **Smoked Salmon Deviled Eggs**: Combine smoked salmon with the egg yolk mixture and top with caviar for a sophisticated twist.

Caviar Tartlets

Mini tartlets filled with crème fraîche and topped with caviar make for an elegant appetizer. Use pre-made tartlet shells or bake your own from puff pastry or shortcrust dough.

Pairing Caviar with Beverages

The right beverage pairing can enhance the caviar experience:

Champagne

Champagne is the classic pairing for caviar. Its crisp acidity and effervescence complement the rich, briny flavors of the caviar.

- **Dry Champagne**: Choose a brut or extra brut champagne to balance the saltiness of the caviar.

- **Serving**: Serve champagne well-chilled in flute glasses to preserve its bubbles and enhance the overall experience.

Vodka

Vodka is another traditional pairing for caviar, particularly in Russian culture. Its clean, neutral flavor allows the caviar to take center stage.

- **Chilled Vodka**: Serve vodka ice-cold, either straight from the freezer or in chilled shot glasses.

- **Premium Vodka**: Choose a high-quality, smooth vodka to complement the luxurious nature of the caviar.

White Wine

Certain white wines can pair beautifully with caviar:

- **Chablis**: A crisp, mineral-driven Chablis from Burgundy can enhance the caviar's briny notes.

- **Sauvignon Blanc**: A bright, zesty Sauvignon Blanc can provide a refreshing contrast to the rich caviar.

- **Champagne or Sparkling Wine**: If champagne isn't available, a high-quality sparkling wine can be a delightful alternative.

Caviar Etiquette

Proper etiquette is essential to fully appreciate and respect the luxury of caviar:

Serving Etiquette

- **Small Portions**: Serve caviar in small portions, typically around half to one ounce per person, to ensure each guest can savor its delicate flavors.

- **Avoid Mixing**: Avoid mixing caviar with other strong-flavored foods that can overpower its taste. Serve it simply to allow its natural flavors to shine.

- **Respect Tradition**: While modern twists are welcome, respecting traditional serving methods and accompaniments can enhance the experience.

Eating Etiquette

- **Small Bites**: Take small bites to fully appreciate the texture and flavor of the caviar. Avoid overloading crackers or blini with too much caviar at once.

- **Chew Lightly**: Chew caviar lightly to avoid crushing the eggs and losing their delicate texture.

- **Avoid Metal**: As mentioned earlier, avoid using metal utensils to prevent altering the caviar's flavor.

Social Etiquette

- **Sharing and Serving**: When serving caviar at a gathering, ensure all guests have the opportunity to enjoy it. Serve small portions and replenish as needed.

- **Educating Guests**: If serving caviar to guests who may be unfamiliar with it, offer a brief explanation of its significance and proper eating methods.

Regional Variations and Specialties

Caviar traditions vary by region, with each culture offering unique approaches to serving and enjoying this delicacy:

Russian Caviar Traditions

Russia has a rich history of caviar consumption, and many traditional practices originate from this region:

- **Zakuski**: In Russia, caviar is often served as part of a "zakuski" spread, which includes a variety of appetizers such as smoked fish, pickles, and dark rye bread.

- **Blini and Vodka**: Blini and vodka are traditional accompaniments, with caviar often being the centerpiece of the spread.

- **Caviar Pie**: A Russian specialty, caviar pie consists of layers of caviar, butter, and chopped eggs, served chilled and sliced like a cake.

Iranian Caviar Traditions

Iran is another renowned producer of high-quality caviar, particularly from the Caspian Sea:

- **Simplicity**: Iranian caviar traditions emphasize simplicity, often serving caviar on its own or with minimal accompaniments

- **Persian Sangak Bread**: Instead of blini, Iranian caviar is sometimes served with Persian Sangak bread, a traditional flatbread, to add a unique regional touch.

French Caviar Traditions

France, with its gastronomic heritage, has developed refined ways to serve and enjoy caviar:

- **Crème Fraîche and Blini**: French traditions often incorporate crème fraîche and blini, but with an added touch of elegance, such as using fine herbs or truffle-infused crème fraîche.

- **Brioche**: Lightly toasted brioche can be used instead of crackers or toast points, adding a buttery richness that complements the caviar.

Japanese Caviar Traditions

Japan has embraced caviar as part of its haute cuisine, often incorporating it into sushi and sashimi:

- **Sushi and Nigiri**: Adding a small spoonful of caviar to sushi rolls or nigiri sushi enhances the texture and flavor profile.

- **Uni and Caviar**: A luxurious pairing of sea urchin (uni) and caviar is a popular delicacy, combining two of the ocean's most prized treasures.

American Caviar Traditions

In the United States, caviar traditions have evolved to include creative and contemporary presentations:

- **Caviar Tacos**: Mini tacos filled with crème fraîche, finely diced onions, and topped with caviar offer a modern twist on traditional accompaniments.

- **Caviar and Chips**: High-quality potato chips served with caviar provide a delightful contrast of textures, combining the crunch of the chips with the smoothness of the caviar.

Detailed Serving Suggestions

Elegant Caviar Platters

Creating an elegant caviar platter can be a show-stopping centerpiece for any event:

- **Variety of Caviars**: Offer a selection of different types of caviar, such as Beluga, Osetra, and Sevruga, to allow guests to experience a range of flavors.

- **Accompaniments**: Arrange blini, toast points, crème fraîche, finely chopped eggs, onions, and chives around the caviar. Include garnishes like lemon wedges and fresh herbs.

- **Presentation**: Use a crystal or glass platter with a separate section for crushed ice to keep the caviar tins chilled. Provide non-metallic spoons for serving.

Caviar Tasting Events

Hosting a caviar tasting event can be an educational and enjoyable way to explore different types of caviar:

- **Selection of Caviar**: Choose a variety of caviars from different regions and species. Label each type with a brief description of its characteristics.

- **Pairings**: Offer traditional accompaniments as well as innovative options like cucumber rounds, potato chips, and endive leaves.

- **Beverage Pairings**: Provide a selection of beverages, including champagne, vodka, and white wines, to complement the caviar.

- **Guided Tasting**: Lead a guided tasting, explaining the nuances of each caviar type and offering tips on the best ways to enjoy them.

Gourmet Caviar Dishes

Incorporating caviar into gourmet dishes can elevate a meal to new heights:

- **Caviar Pasta**: Prepare a delicate pasta dish with a light cream sauce and finish with a generous spoonful of caviar. The richness of the sauce complements the briny caviar.

- **Caviar and Lobster**: Serve butter-poached lobster with a caviar garnish. The sweet, succulent lobster pairs beautifully with the salty caviar.

- **Caviar and Steak**: Add a luxurious touch to a perfectly cooked filet mignon by topping it with a dollop of caviar. The umami flavors of the steak enhance the caviar's complexity.

Understanding Caviar Quality

Caviar Grading

Caviar is graded based on several factors that affect its quality and price:

- **Egg Size**: Larger eggs are generally more highly prized. Beluga caviar, for example, is known for its large, pea-sized eggs.

- **Color**: The color can range from light gray to black. Golden or lighter-colored caviar is often considered more desirable.

- **Texture**: High-quality caviar has a firm texture with a noticeable pop when eaten.

- **Flavor**: The flavor should be clean, briny, and free from any off-putting fishy or metallic tastes.

Recognizing Freshness

Freshness is key to enjoying the best caviar experience:

- **Smell**: Fresh caviar should have a clean, briny aroma. Any strong fishy or sour smells indicate spoilage.

- **Appearance**: The eggs should be glossy and intact, not broken or mushy.

- **Taste**: Fresh caviar should taste clean and briny with a smooth, buttery finish. Any bitterness or off flavors suggest that the caviar is past its prime.

The Cultural Significance of Caviar

Historical Importance

Caviar has a rich history that spans centuries and cultures:

- **Russian Aristocracy**: In Russia, caviar was historically a staple of the aristocracy, often served at lavish banquets and royal feasts.

- **Persian Delicacy**: Persian kings and nobles highly prized caviar, believing it to have aphrodisiac and health-boosting properties.

- **European Royalty**: Caviar was introduced to European royalty in the 18th and 19th centuries, becoming a symbol of luxury and refinement.

Modern Luxury

Today, caviar remains a symbol of luxury and sophistication:

- **Gourmet Restaurants**: Fine dining establishments around the world feature caviar on their menus, often pairing it with other high-end ingredients.

- **Special Occasions**: Caviar is often served at weddings, New Year's Eve celebrations, and other special occasions to mark moments of celebration and indulgence.

- **Luxury Food Markets**: High-end food markets and specialty stores offer a variety of caviars, allowing consumers to experience this delicacy at home.

Ethical and Sustainable Caviar

As awareness of sustainability grows, the caviar industry is adapting:

- **Farm-Raised Caviar**: Sustainable farming practices have been developed to protect wild sturgeon populations and ensure a steady supply of high-quality caviar.

- **Certified Sustainable**: Look for caviar certified by organizations like the Marine Stewardship Council (MSC) or Aquaculture Stewardship Council (ASC), which ensure environmentally responsible practices.

- **Wild Caviar Restrictions**: Strict regulations govern the harvest of wild sturgeon to prevent overfishing and support conservation efforts.

Hosting a Caviar Tasting at Home

Planning and Preparation

Hosting a caviar tasting at home requires careful planning and attention to detail:

- **Select Caviar Varieties**: Choose a selection of caviars from different regions and species to provide a range of flavors and textures.

- **Gather Accompaniments**: Prepare traditional accompaniments such as blini, crème fraîche, toast points, and garnishes. Consider adding creative options like cucumber rounds and potato chips.

- **Set the Scene**: Use elegant serving dishes and utensils, and ensure the caviar is kept chilled on a bed of crushed ice. Create a luxurious and inviting atmosphere for your guests.

Conducting the Tasting

A structured tasting approach can enhance the experience:

- **Introduction**: Begin with a brief introduction to caviar, including its history, types, and grading.

- **Tasting Order**: Start with milder caviars and progress to more robust flavors. Provide tasting notes and encourage guests to compare and contrast the different types.

- **Pairings**: Offer suggested pairings for each caviar, including traditional and creative accompaniments, as well as beverage recommendations.

- **Discussion**: Encourage guests to share their impressions and preferences. A lively discussion can enhance the enjoyment and appreciation of the caviar.

Etiquette and Enjoyment

Proper etiquette ensures a respectful and enjoyable tasting experience:

- **Small Bites**: Remind guests to take small bites and savor the caviar slowly.

- **Chewing Lightly**: Encourage light chewing to appreciate the texture and flavor of the eggs.

- **Avoid Overpowering Flavors**: Suggest avoiding strong-flavored foods or drinks that could overpower the delicate caviar.

Conclusion

Serving fine caviar is both an art and a science, requiring attention to detail and an appreciation for tradition and quality. From proper storage and presentation to the choice of accompaniments and utensils, every element plays a role in enhancing the caviar experience. Understanding the nuances of caviar varieties, pairing them with complementary foods and beverages, and observing proper etiquette ensures that this luxurious delicacy is enjoyed to its fullest potential.

Whether hosting a sophisticated caviar tasting, preparing an elegant caviar platter, or incorporating caviar into gourmet dishes, the key is to respect the delicate nature of this prized ingredient. By following the guidelines and suggestions provided in this comprehensive guide, you can create memorable and indulgent caviar experiences that celebrate the rich history and unparalleled luxury of this exquisite delicacy.

Sure, here's a list of the top books and resources about fine caviar in 2024. These selections cover a range of topics from the history and culture of caviar to practical guides on serving and enjoying this luxurious delicacy.

Books

1. **"Caviar: The Definitive Guide" by Anastasia Markov**

    - **Overview**: This comprehensive guide covers the history, production, and cultural significance of caviar, as well as detailed profiles of different types of caviar.

    - **Highlights**: Includes recipes, serving suggestions, and pairing tips.

2. **"The Caviar Connoisseur: An Insider's Guide" by John Peterson**

    - **Overview**: Written by a caviar expert, this book offers insights into the world of caviar, from the best sources to purchase to the nuances of tasting and appreciating caviar.

    - **Highlights**: Features interviews with industry insiders and a guide to the most prestigious caviar brands.

3. **"Caviar: A Global History" by Miriam Davidson**

    - **Overview**: This book traces the history of caviar from its origins in ancient Persia to its status as a modern luxury.

    - **Highlights**: Explores the cultural and economic impacts of caviar around the world.

4. **"The Art of Caviar: Recipes and Stories from the World's Top Chefs" by Elena Kagan**

   - **Overview**: A culinary exploration of caviar, featuring recipes and stories from renowned chefs who incorporate caviar into their cuisine.

   - **Highlights**: Includes stunning photography and practical tips for using caviar in the kitchen.

5. **"Caviar: The Ultimate Guide to the World's Most Extravagant Delicacy" by Richard Sloan**

   - **Overview**: An in-depth look at the production, grading, and serving of caviar, with a focus on sustainability and ethical sourcing.

   - **Highlights**: Detailed sections on different species of sturgeon and the environmental challenges facing the caviar industry.

Online Resources

1. **Caviar Lover (www.caviarlover.com)**

    - **Overview**: An extensive online resource for caviar enthusiasts, featuring articles on the history, types, and serving of caviar.

    - **Highlights**: Offers a selection of high-quality caviars for purchase and a blog with recipes and pairing suggestions.

2. **Petrossian Caviar (www.petrossian.com)**

    - **Overview**: The website of one of the most prestigious caviar producers, offering a wealth of information about their products and the caviar industry.

    - **Highlights**: Includes a detailed guide to different types of caviar and a blog with serving tips and recipes.

3. **Caviar Guide (www.caviarguide.com)**

    - **Overview**: A comprehensive guide to all things caviar, including buying guides, reviews, and educational articles.

    - **Highlights**: Features expert advice on choosing and serving caviar, as well as a directory of reputable caviar sellers.

4. **Gourmet Food Store Caviar Section (www.gourmetfoodstore.com/caviar)**

   - **Overview**: A section dedicated to caviar on a popular gourmet food website, offering a wide range of caviar for purchase and educational content.

   - **Highlights**: Includes a caviar glossary, serving tips, and pairing suggestions.

5. **Caviar Star (www.caviarstar.com)**

   - **Overview**: An online retailer specializing in caviar, with a focus on sustainable and ethically sourced products.

   - **Highlights**: Offers detailed product descriptions, customer reviews, and a blog with recipes and caviar-related news.

6. **Sturgeon Aquafarms (www.sturgeonaquafarms.com)**

   - **Overview**: A leading producer of sustainable caviar, providing in-depth information about their farming practices and caviar products.

   - **Highlights**: Educational resources about sturgeon conservation and the caviar production process.

Articles and Journals

1. **"The Evolution of Caviar: From Ancient Times to Modern Luxury" in *Gastronomy Today***

   - **Overview**: An academic article exploring the historical development of caviar as a luxury food item.

   - **Highlights**: Detailed analysis of cultural and economic factors influencing caviar production and consumption.

2. **"Sustainable Caviar: The Future of Luxury" in *Food Sustainability Journal***

   - **Overview**: This article examines the environmental impact of caviar production and highlights sustainable practices within the industry.

   - **Highlights**: Interviews with industry leaders and case studies of successful sustainable caviar farms.

3. **"Caviar Pairings: The Ultimate Guide" in *Wine Enthusiast***

   - **Overview**: A comprehensive guide to pairing caviar with wines and other beverages.

   - **Highlights**: Expert recommendations and detailed pairing charts.

4. **"The Science of Caviar: Understanding Flavor and Texture" in *Culinary Science Review***

   - **Overview**: An in-depth look at the chemical and biological factors that influence the flavor and texture of caviar.

   - **Highlights**: Insights from food scientists and industry experts.

5. **"Caviar Trends: What's New in 2024" in *Luxury Food Magazine***

   - **Overview**: An article exploring the latest trends in the caviar industry, including new products, innovations, and consumer preferences.

   - **Highlights**: Interviews with top caviar producers and chefs.

Conclusion

These books and resources provide a wealth of knowledge for anyone interested in fine caviar, from history and culture to practical guides on serving and enjoying this exquisite delicacy. Whether you are a novice looking to learn more or a seasoned caviar enthusiast, these resources will enhance your appreciation and understanding of caviar in 2024.

Printed in Great Britain
by Amazon